CLIMATE CHANGE

Crown of Thorns Starfish

By Jordon Mooka

I0158300

We respect and honour Aboriginal and Torres Strait Islander Elders past, present and future. We acknowledge the stories, traditions and living cultures of Aboriginal and Torres Strait Islander peoples on this land and commit to building a brighter future together.

Library For All Ltd.

What is Climate Change?

Climate change means that the Earth's weather patterns and temperatures are changing. These changes mostly come from people's actions, like burning oil and coal, which releases gases that warm up the planet.

The sun's rays warm the earth.

Burning fuels and other pollutants cause a greenhouse effect in our atmosphere.

Some heat should stay within our atmosphere, but some escapes into space.

More heat stays on Earth, so temperatures rise and weather patterns change. We get stronger storms, heavier rain and longer droughts.

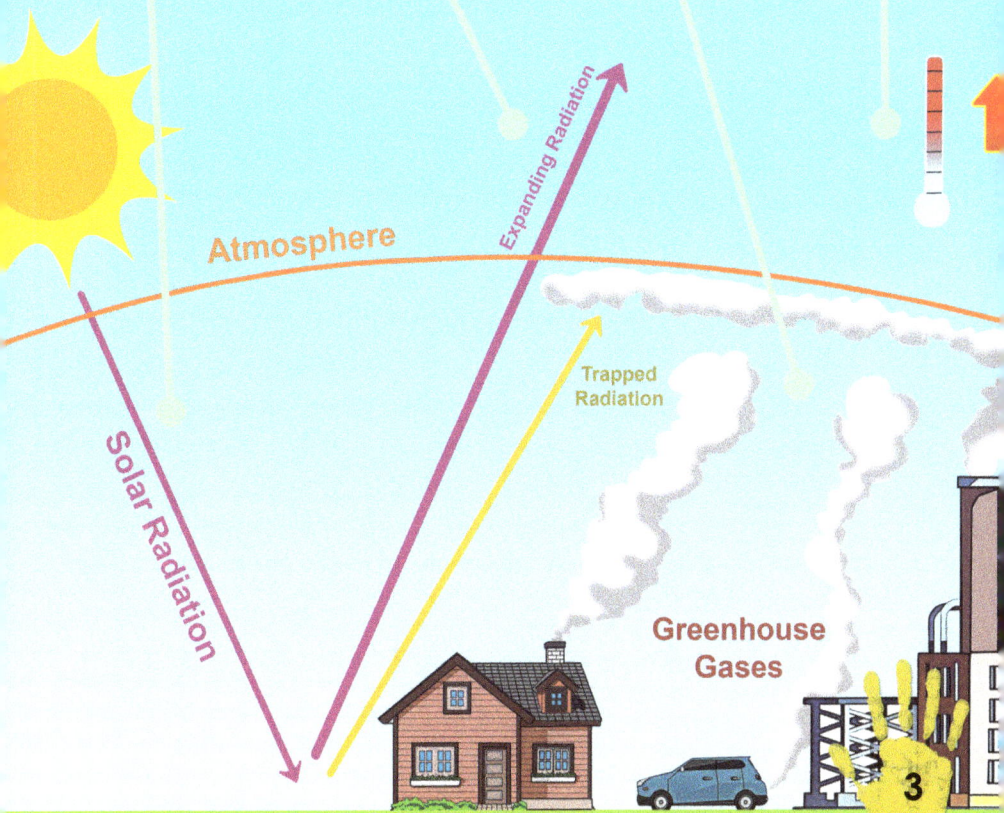

Expanding Radiation

Atmosphere

Trapped Radiation

Solar Radiation

Greenhouse Gases

3

What are Crown of Thorns Starfish?

Who is this poisonous predator?

The Crown of Thorns starfish is a Great Barrier Reef native that often stirs up trouble. These starfish can have up to 21 arms, and their bodies and arms are covered in toxic thorns to deter any curious predators. Each spike is around 4cm long and can cause serious illness in humans and other animals.

Despite being able to grow up to 80cm in diameter, Crown of Thorns starfish are excellent hiders. When not feeding, they prefer dark corners or the undersides of ledges. They appear in several different colours, including purple, brown, green, or grey, and their spines can be red, yellow, blue, or brown.

So, what makes them dangerous?

The Crown of Thorns starfish eats hard coral, stripping it of its living tissue. Large numbers of these starfish can destroy an entire reef, and due to coral bleaching and water pollution, those coral reefs struggle to recover.

Climate change causes severe stress on coral reefs worldwide.

Crown of Thorns starfish outbreaks are serious environmental disasters. An outbreak is declared when there are 15 or more of these starfish in a coral reef.

Crown of Thorns, Climate Change, and the Reef

Climate change has seriously negative effects on the Great Barrier Reef and reefs worldwide. Due to changes in weather patterns, more frequent natural disasters, and rising ocean temperatures, coral reefs are bleaching from ecosystem stress.

Normally, Crown of Thorns starfish are a key part of the ecosystem. They eat fast-growing coral, allowing slow-growing coral to catch up and not be overtaken.

Now that coral reefs are bleaching, these starfish are a threat to their recovery.

Crown of Thorns, Climate Change, and the Reef

Crown of Thorns exacerbate the damage done to reefs by climate change, eating already stressed and weakened coral. This irreversibly destabilises the reef structure and destroys ecological harmony.

What happens to the coral?

After bleaching and Crown
of Thorns starfish are done with it, coral reefs
are damaged and discoloured. They exist only
as 'skeletons', which is the term for white,
lifeless coral. They no longer provide homes
and food for other marine life.

Despite Crown of Thorns always existing on
the reefs, human interference has changed
the frequency of these outbreaks and further
pressured the coral.

Combating Crown of Thorns

Indigenous rangers use traditional methods and modern techniques together to manage starfish outbreaks and keep the reef healthy. But starfish management is delicate and time consuming.

DID YOU KNOW?

In an outbreak, starfish can number in the tens of thousands on a single reef!

Monitoring is done by divers using manta-tows – like underwater clipboards towed behind a boat. When an outbreak is discovered, starfish are injected with vinegar, which destroys them. This controls immediate numbers and disrupts the breeding cycle.

Cultural Impacts and Community Responses

Traditional stories that involve the Crown of Thorns starfish articulate the interconnectedness of natural phenomena and cultural values, guiding current conservation strategies and emphasizing the importance of a healthy reef for cultural continuity.

Connection to Country

The degradation of reefs affects biodiversity but also the cultural fabric of Indigenous communities that are deeply connected to the reef. Girringun Rangers and traditional owners actively participate in the monitoring and recovery of the reef. Seasonal hunting bans, cultural burns, and other traditional practices are employed, showcasing a holistic approach to environmental stewardship.

Environmental stewardship means caring for the reef now and into the future.

Fantastic Facts!

Secrets of the Crown of Thorns Starfish

1 These starfish breed easily, with females releasing over 60 million eggs in one spawning season.

They can consume up to 10 square metres of coral every year.

3 Crown of Thorns outbreaks are caused by increased nutrients in the water and the removal of predators.

Natural predators include giant triton snails, starry pufferfish, titan trigger fish, and humphead maori wrasse.

5

Crown of Thorns starfish eat by pushing their stomachs out of their bodies, wrapping it around coral, and digesting the tissue.

These starfish are some of the largest in the world!

7

They are nocturnal creatures and can move up to 20 metres an hour.

The Biggest Coral Colony

One of the biggest coral colonies ever recorded is a massive Porites coral in the Great Barrier Reef, measuring about 10 metres high and 20 metres wide. Imagine how many sea creatures would be impacted if all of that coral was bleached?

Do the Reef Quiz

Q What causes global warming?

A Pollution, like carbon dioxide, keeps heat close to Earth, like a greenhouse.

Q How does climate change affect reefs?

A It makes the ocean too warm.

Q What causes coral bleaching?

A When the ocean gets warm, coral expels helpful algae.

Q Why is coral bleaching a problem?

A Bleached coral is fragile and disease prone.

Q How does an unhealthy reef impact marine life?

A Sea creatures lose their home and food source.

Q How does an unhealthy reef impact humans?

A It reduces fishing and tourism, and increases coastal erosion.

Q How do Rangers help the reef?

A They watch carefully, make records, and limit hunting and tourism.

Q How can you help the reef?

A Try to save energy and talk to people around you about ways to help stop pollution.

19

Photo Credits

Page	Attribution
Cover	Horizon International Images/Alamy Stock Photo
Pages 2	ArliftAtoz2205/Shutterstock.com
Page 3	© Library For All
Page 4	Minden Pictures / Alamy Stock Photo
Page 5 (above)	Tropic Pixel/Shutterstock.com
Page 5 (below)	Andrea Izzotti/Shutterstock.com
Page 6	Ethan Daniels/Shutterstock.com
Page 7	Minden Pictures / Alamy Stock Photo
Page 8-9	Ethan Daniels/Shutterstock.com
Page 10	cdelacy/Shutterstock.com
Page 11	Davdeka/Shuterstock.com
Page 12–13	© Library For All
Page 14	Photo courtesy of the Queensland Indigenous Land and Sea Ranger Program.
Page 15	Serhiy Buslenko/Shutterstock.com
Page 16	Ethan Daniels/Shutterstock.com
Page 17 (above)	Peter Douglas Clark/Shutterstock.com
Page 17 (below)	vkilikov/Shutterstock.com
Page 18	Suzanne Long / Alamy Stock Photo
Page 19	© Library For All

You can use these questions to talk about this book with your family, friends and teachers.

What did you learn from this book?

Describe this book in one word. Funny? Scary? Colourful? Interesting?

How did this book make you feel when you finished reading it?

What was your favourite part of this book?

Download the Library For All Reader app from libraryforall.org

Queensland Indigenous Land and Sea Ranger Program

The Queensland Indigenous Land and Sea Ranger Program collaborates with First Nations communities to protect and care for land and sea Country. With over 200 rangers, the program shares cultural knowledge, engages in community education, and leads youth programs like the Junior Ranger initiative, fostering a strong connection to Country and Culture.

Jordan Mooka is a Girringun Ranger of the Cardwell community.

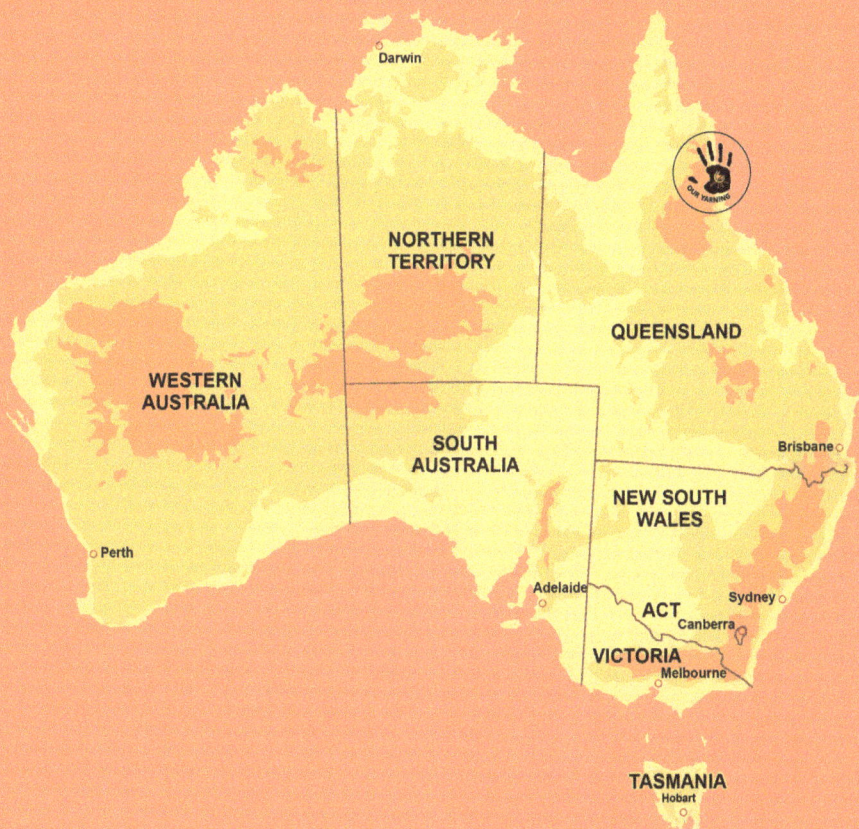

Darwin

NORTHERN
TERRITORY

QUEENSLAND

WESTERN
AUSTRALIA

SOUTH
AUSTRALIA

Brisbane

NEW SOUTH
WALES

Perth

Adelaide

Sydney

ACT
Canberra

VICTORIA
Melbourne

TASMANIA
Hobart

Our Yarning

The Our Yarning collection aligns with the Australian Curriculum through the Cross-Curriculum Priorities — Aboriginal and Torres Strait Islander Histories and Cultures. The collection provides an authentic opportunity for learning and embedding Aboriginal and Torres Strait Islander perspectives because it is written by Aboriginal and Torres Strait Islander people.

We know that children learn better, and enjoy reading more, when they see themselves in the stories, characters and illustrations of the books they read.

To download the app, visit the Google Play Store or Apple Store and search 'Our Yarning'.

libraryforall.org

You're reading Upper Primary

Learner – Beginner readers

Start your reading journey with short words, big ideas and plenty of pictures.

Level 1 – Rising readers

Raise your reading level with more words, simple sentences and exciting images.

Level 2 – Eager readers

Enjoy your reading time with familiar words, but complex sentences.

Level 3 – Progressing readers

Develop your reading skills with creative stories and some challenging vocabulary.

Level 4 – Fluent readers

Step up your reading skills with playful narratives, new words and fun facts.

Middle Primary – Curious readers

Discover your world through science and stories.

Upper Primary – Adventurous readers

Explore your world through science and stories.

Library For All is an Australian not for profit organisation with a mission to make knowledge accessible to all via an innovative digital library solution.
Visit us at libraryforall.org

Climate Change: Crown of Thorns Starfish

First published 2024

Published by Library For All Ltd
Email: info@libraryforall.org
URL: libraryforall.org

This work is licensed under the Creative Commons Attribution-NonCommercial-NoDerivatives 4.0 International License. To view a copy of this license, visit http://creativecommons.org/licenses/by-nc-nd/4.0/.

This project was delivered with the support of QBE under the Community Ready partnership.

Community
Ready

This book was made possible with the support of the Queensland Indigenous Land and Sea Ranger Program to support educational outcomes for children in Australia by learning from Indigenous knowledge and stewardship of Country. To learn more, visit https://www.qld.gov.au/environment/plants-animals/conservation/community/land-sea-rangers/locations.

Our Yarning logo design by Jason Lee, Bidjipidji Art

Climate Change: Crown of Thorns Starfish
Mooka, Jordon
ISBN: 978-1-923207-48-6
SKU04434